CHRISTMAS HITS FOR TWO

ISBN 978-1-4950-6921-5

HAL•LEONARD®
CORPORATION
7777 W. BLUEMOUND RD. P.O. BOX 13819 MILWAUKEE, WI 53213

For all works contained herein:
Unauthorized copying, arranging, adapting, recording, Internet posting, public performance,
or other distribution of the printed music in this publication is an infringement of copyright.
Infringers are liable under the law.

Visit Hal Leonard Online at
www.halleonard.com

CONTENTS

ALL I WANT FOR CHRISTMAS IS YOU

TROMBONES

Words and Music by MARIAH CAREY
and WALTER AFANASIEFF

Copyright © 1994 BEYONDIDOLIZATION, SONY/ATV MUSIC PUBLISHING LLC, TAMAL VISTA MUSIC,
WALLYWORLD MUSIC and KOBALT MUSIC COPYRIGHTS SARL
All Rights for BEYONDIDOLIZATION Controlled and Administered by UNIVERSAL TUNES, A Division of SONGS OF UNIVERSAL, INC.
All Rights for SONY/ATV MUSIC PUBLISHING LLC, TAMAL VISTA MUSIC and WALLYWORLD MUSIC Administered by
SONY/ATV MUSIC PUBLISHING LLC, 424 Church Street, Suite 1200, Nashville, TN 37219
All Rights Reserved   Used by Permission

BABY, IT'S COLD OUTSIDE

from the Motion Picture NEPTUNE'S DAUGHTER

TROMBONES

By FRANK LOESSER

© 1948 (Renewed) FRANK MUSIC CORP.
All Rights Reserved

THE CHRISTMAS SONG
(Chestnuts Roasting on an Open Fire)

TROMBONES

Music and Lyric by MEL TORMÉ
and ROBERT WELLS

Moderately slow

© 1946 (Renewed) EDWIN H. MORRIS & COMPANY, A Division of MPL Music Publishing, Inc. and SONY/ATV MUSIC PUBLISHING LLC
All Rights on behalf of SONY/ATV MUSIC PUBLISHING LLC Administered by
SONY/ATV MUSIC PUBLISHING LLC, 424 Church Street, Suite 1200, Nashville, TN 37219
All Rights Reserved

THE CHRISTMAS WALTZ

TROMBONES

Words by SAMMY CAHN
Music by JULE STYNE

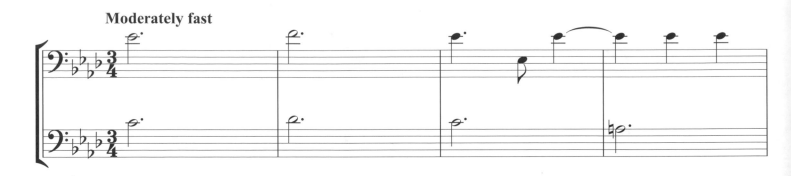

© 1954 (Renewed) PRODUCERS MUSIC PUBLISHING CO., INC. and CAHN MUSIC CO.
All Rights for PRODUCERS MUSIC PUBLISHING CO., INC. Administered by CHAPPELL & CO., INC.
All Rights for CAHN MUSIC CO. Administered by IMAGEM SOUNDS
All Rights Reserved   Used by Permission

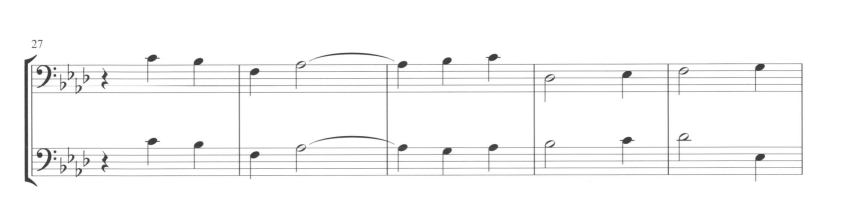

DO YOU HEAR WHAT I HEAR

TROMBONES

Words and Music by NOEL REGNEY
and GLORIA SHAYNE

Moderately

Copyright © 1962 (Renewed) by Jewel Music Publishing Co., Inc. (ASCAP)
International Copyright Secured   All Rights Reserved
Used by Permission

DO YOU WANT TO BUILD A SNOWMAN?

from FROZEN

TROMBONES

Music and Lyrics by KRISTEN ANDERSON-LOPEZ
and ROBERT LOPEZ

Moderately fast

© 2013 Wonderland Music Company, Inc.
All Rights Reserved. Used by Permission.

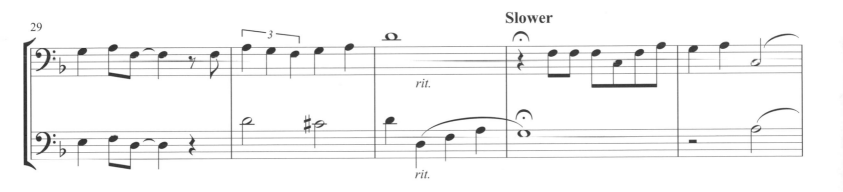

FELIZ NAVIDAD

TROMBONES

Music and Lyrics by
JOSÉ FELICIANO

Moderately

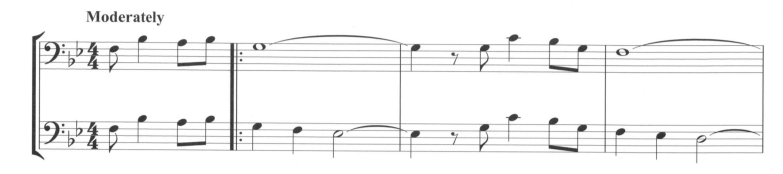

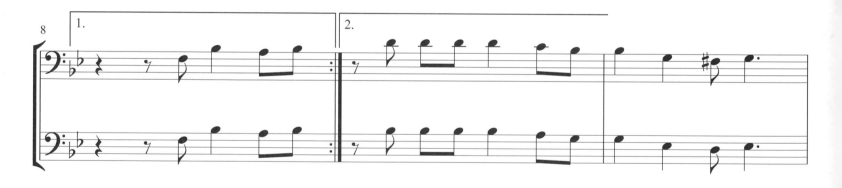

Copyright © 1970 J & H Publishing Company (ASCAP)
Copyright Renewed
All Rights Administered by Law, P.A. o/b/o J & H Publishing Company
International Copyright Secured   All Rights Reserved

HAVE YOURSELF A MERRY LITTLE CHRISTMAS

from MEET ME IN ST. LOUIS

TROMBONES

Words and Music by HUGH MARTIN
and RALPH BLANE

Moderately slow

© 1943 (Renewed) METRO-GOLDWYN-MAYER INC.
© 1944 (Renewed) EMI FEIST CATALOG INC.
All Rights Controlled and Administered by EMI FEIST CATALOG INC. (Publishing) and ALFRED MUSIC (Print)
All Rights Reserved   Used by Permission

HERE COMES SANTA CLAUS
(Right Down Santa Claus Lane)

TROMBONES

Words and Music by GENE AUTRY
and OAKLEY HALDEMAN

© 1947 (Renewed) Gene Autry's Western Music Publishing Co.
All Rights Reserved   Used by Permission

A HOLLY JOLLY CHRISTMAS

TROMBONES

Music and Lyrics by
JOHNNY MARKS

Moderately bright

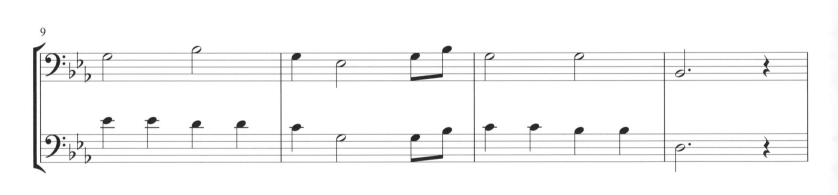

Copyright © 1962, 1964 (Renewed 1990, 1992) St. Nicholas Music Inc., 254 W. 54th Street, 12th Floor, New York, New York 10019
All Rights Reserved

(There's No Place Like)

HOME FOR THE HOLIDAYS

TROMBONES

Words and Music by AL STILLMAN
and ROBERT ALLEN

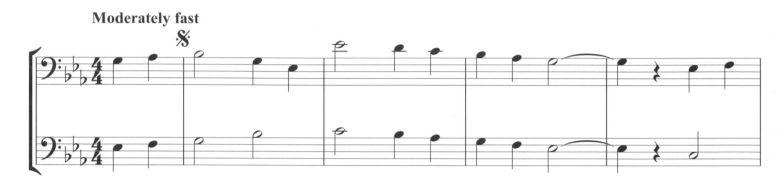

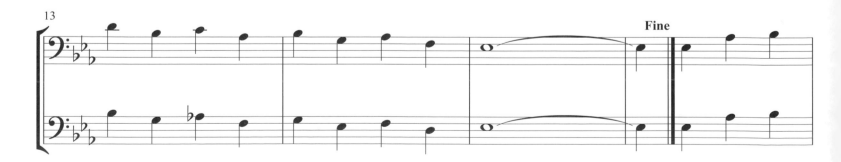

© Copyright 1954 (Renewed) by Music Sales Corporation (ASCAP) and Charlie Deitcher Productions
International Copyright Secured   All Rights Reserved   Used by Permission

D.S. al Fine

I'LL BE HOME FOR CHRISTMAS

TROMBONES

Words and Music by KIM GANNON
and WALTER KENT

Moderately

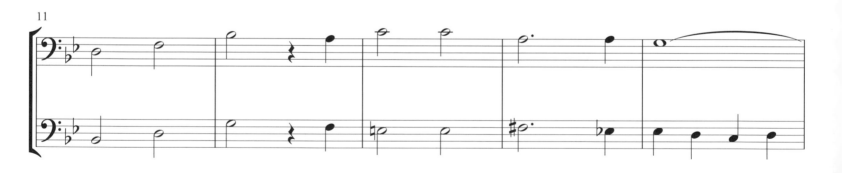

© Copyright 1943 by Gannon & Kent Music Co., Inc., Beverly Hills, CA
Copyright Renewed
International Copyright Secured   All Rights Reserved

IT'S BEGINNING TO LOOK LIKE CHRISTMAS

TROMBONES

By MEREDITH WILLSON

© 1951 PLYMOUTH MUSIC CO., INC.
© Renewed 1979 FRANK MUSIC CORP. and MEREDITH WILLSON MUSIC
All Rights Reserved

LET IT SNOW! LET IT SNOW! LET IT SNOW!

TROMBONES

Words by SAMMY CAHN
Music by JULE STYNE

© 1945 (Renewed) PRODUCERS MUSIC PUBLISHING CO., INC. and CAHN MUSIC CO.
All Rights for PRODUCERS MUSIC PUBLISHING CO., INC. Administered by CHAPPELL & CO., INC.
All Rights for CAHN MUSIC CO. Administered by IMAGEM SOUNDS
All Rights Reserved   Used by Permission

MARY, DID YOU KNOW?

TROMBONES

Words and Music by MARK LOWRY
and BUDDY GREENE

© 1991 Word Music, LLC and Rufus Music (administered at CapitolCMGPublishing.com)
All Rights Reserved   Used by Permission

THE MOST WONDERFUL TIME OF THE YEAR

TROMBONES

Words and Music by EDDIE POLA
and GEORGE WYLE

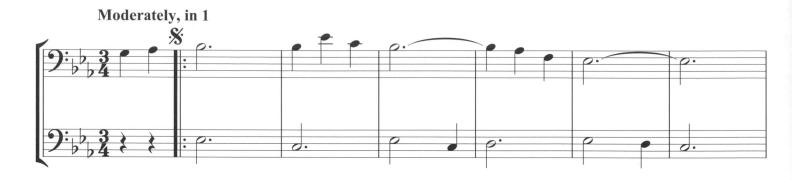

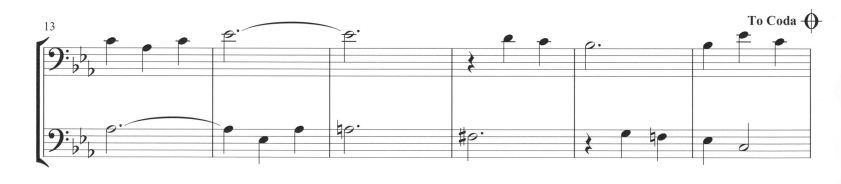

Copyright © 1963 Barnaby Music Corp.
Copyright Renewed
Administered by Lichelle Music Company
International Copyright Secured   All Rights Reserved

MY FAVORITE THINGS

from THE SOUND OF MUSIC

TROMBONES

Lyrics by OSCAR HAMMERSTEIN II
Music by RICHARD RODGERS

Copyright © 1959 by Richard Rodgers and Oscar Hammerstein II
Copyright Renewed
Williamson Music, a Division of Rodgers & Hammerstein: an Imagem Company, owner of publication and allied rights throughout the world
International Copyright Secured   All Rights Reserved

ROCKIN' AROUND THE CHRISTMAS TREE

TROMBONES

Music and Lyrics by
JOHNNY MARKS

Copyright © 1958 (Renewed 1986) St. Nicholas Music Inc., 254 W. 54th Street, 12th Floor, New York, New York 10019
All Rights Reserved

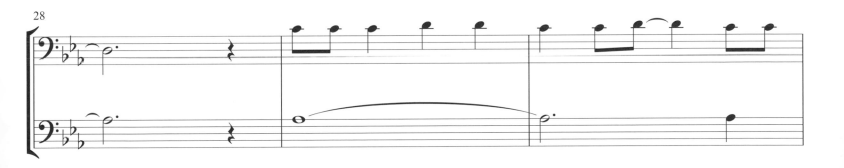

RUDOLPH THE RED-NOSED REINDEER

TROMBONES

Music and Lyrics by
JOHNNY MARKS

Copyright © 1949 (Renewed 1977) St. Nicholas Music Inc., 254 W. 54th Street, 12th Floor, New York, New York 10019
All Rights Reserved

SILVER BELLS
from the Paramount Picture THE LEMON DROP KID

TROMBONES

Words and Music by JAY LIVINGSTON
and RAY EVANS

Moderately

Copyright © 1950 Sony/ATV Music Publishing LLC
Copyright Renewed
All Rights Administered by Sony/ATV Music Publishing LLC, 424 Church Street, Suite 1200, Nashville, TN 37219
International Copyright Secured   All Rights Reserved

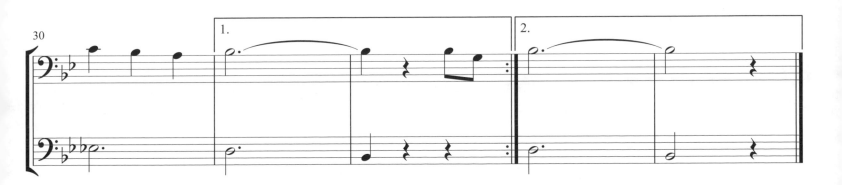

SOMEWHERE IN MY MEMORY

from the Twentieth Century Fox Motion Picture HOME ALONE

TROMBONES

Words by LESLIE BRICUSSE
Music by JOHN WILLIAMS

Copyright © 1990 Fox Film Music Corporation and John Hughes Songs
All Rights for John Hughes Songs Administered by Warner-Tamerlane Publishing Corp.
All Rights Reserved   Used by Permission

WHITE CHRISTMAS
from the Motion Picture Irving Berlin's HOLIDAY INN

TROMBONES

Words and Music by
IRVING BERLIN

Slowly, in 2

© Copyright 1940, 1942 by Irving Berlin
Copyright Renewed
International Copyright Secured   All Rights Reserved

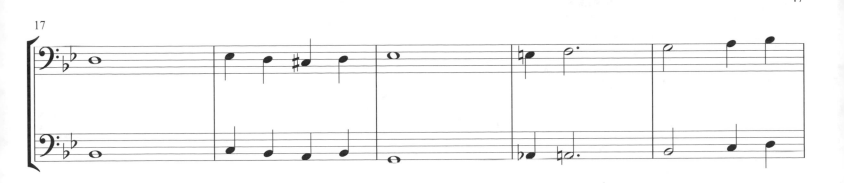

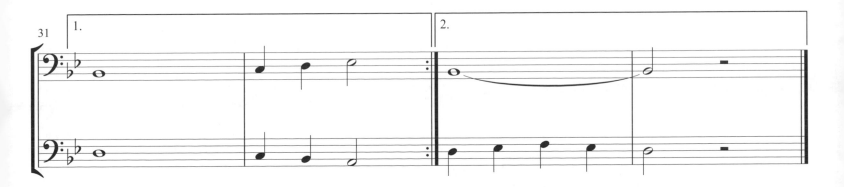

HAL•LEONARD INSTRUMENTAL PLAY-ALONG

Your favorite songs are arranged just for solo instrumentalists with this outstanding series. Each book includes a great full-accompaniment play-along audio so you can sound just like a pro! Check out www.halleonard.com to see all the titles available.

Chart Hits

All About That Bass • All of Me • Happy • Radioactive • Roar • Say Something • Shake It Off • A Sky Full of Stars • Someone like You • Stay with Me • Thinking Out Loud • Uptown Funk.

_____00146207	Flute	$12.99
_____00146208	Clarinet	$12.99
_____00146209	Alto Sax	$12.99
_____00146210	Tenor Sax	$12.99
_____00146211	Trumpet	$12.99
_____00146212	Horn	$12.99
_____00146213	Trombone	$12.99
_____00146214	Violin	$12.99
_____00146215	Viola	$12.99
_____00146216	Cello	$12.99

Coldplay

Clocks • Every Teardrop Is a Waterfall • Fix You • In My Place • Lost! • Paradise • The Scientist • Speed of Sound • Trouble • Violet Hill • Viva La Vida • Yellow.

_____00103337	Flute	$12.99
_____00103338	Clarinet	$12.99
_____00103339	Alto Sax	$12.99
_____00103340	Tenor Sax	$12.99
_____00103341	Trumpet	$12.99
_____00103342	Horn	$12.99
_____00103343	Trombone	$12.99
_____00103344	Violin	$12.99
_____00103345	Viola	$12.99
_____00103346	Cello	$12.99

Disney Greats

Arabian Nights • Hawaiian Roller Coaster Ride • It's a Small World • Look Through My Eyes • Yo Ho (A Pirate's Life for Me) • and more.

_____00841934	Flute	$12.99
_____00841935	Clarinet	$12.99
_____00841936	Alto Sax	$12.99
_____00841937	Tenor Sax	$12.95
_____00841938	Trumpet	$12.99
_____00841939	Horn	$12.95
_____00841940	Trombone	$12.95
_____00841941	Violin	$12.99
_____00841942	Viola	$12.95
_____00841943	Cello	$12.99
_____00842078	Oboe	$12.99

Great Themes

Bella's Lullaby • Chariots of Fire • Get Smart • Hawaii Five-O Theme • I Love Lucy • The Odd Couple • Spanish Flea • and more.

_____00842468	Flute	$12.99
_____00842469	Clarinet	$12.99
_____00842470	Alto Sax	$12.99
_____00842471	Tenor Sax	$12.99
_____00842472	Trumpet	$12.99
_____00842473	Horn	$12.99
_____00842474	Trombone	$12.99
_____00842475	Violin	$12.99
_____00842476	Viola	$12.99
_____00842477	Cello	$12.99

Lennon & McCartney Favorites

All You Need Is Love • A Hard Day's Night • Here, There and Everywhere • Hey Jude • Let It Be • Nowhere Man • Penny Lane • She Loves You • When I'm Sixty-Four • and more.

_____00842600	Flute	$12.99
_____00842601	Clarinet	$12.99
_____00842602	Alto Sax	$12.99
_____00842603	Tenor Sax	$12.99
_____00842604	Trumpet	$12.99
_____00842605	Horn	$12.99
_____00842607	Violin	$12.99
_____00842608	Viola	$12.99
_____00842609	Cello	$12.99

Popular Hits

Breakeven • Fireflies • Halo • Hey, Soul Sister • I Gotta Feeling • I'm Yours • Need You Now • Poker Face • Viva La Vida • You Belong with Me • and more.

_____00842511	Flute	$12.99
_____00842512	Clarinet	$12.99
_____00842513	Alto Sax	$12.99
_____00842514	Tenor Sax	$12.99
_____00842515	Trumpet	$12.99
_____00842516	Horn	$12.99
_____00842517	Trombone	$12.99
_____00842518	Violin	$12.99
_____00842519	Viola	$12.99
_____00842520	Cello	$12.99

Songs from Frozen, Tangled and Enchanted

Do You Want to Build a Snowman? • For the First Time in Forever • Happy Working Song • I See the Light • In Summer • Let It Go • Mother Knows Best • That's How You Know • True Love's First Kiss • When Will My Life Begin • and more.

_____00126921	Flute	$12.99
_____00126922	Clarinet	$12.99
_____00126923	Alto Sax	$12.99
_____00126924	Tenor Sax	$12.99
_____00126925	Trumpet	$12.99
_____00126926	Horn	$12.99
_____00126927	Trombone	$12.99
_____00126928	Violin	$12.99
_____00126929	Viola	$12.99
_____00126930	Cello	$12.99

Women of Pop

Bad Romance • Jar of Hearts • Mean • My Life Would Suck Without You • Our Song • Rolling in the Deep • Single Ladies (Put a Ring on It) • Teenage Dream • and more.

_____00842650	Flute	$12.99
_____00842651	Clarinet	$12.99
_____00842652	Alto Sax	$12.99
_____00842653	Tenor Sax	$12.99
_____00842654	Trumpet	$12.99
_____00842655	Horn	$12.99
_____00842656	Trombone	$12.99
_____00842657	Violin	$12.99
_____00842658	Viola	$12.99
_____00842659	Cello	$12.99

Wicked

As Long As You're Mine • Dancing Through Life • Defying Gravity • For Good • I'm Not That Girl • Popular • The Wizard and I • and more.

_____00842236	Flute	$11.95
_____00842237	Clarinet	$11.99
_____00842238	Alto Saxophone	$11.95
_____00842239	Tenor Saxophone	$11.95
_____00842240	Trumpet	$11.99
_____00842241	Horn	$11.95
_____00842242	Trombone	$11.95
_____00842243	Violin	$11.99
_____00842244	Viola	$11.95
_____00842245	Cello	$11.99

FOR MORE INFORMATION, SEE YOUR LOCAL MUSIC DEALER, OR WRITE TO:

HAL•LEONARD® CORPORATION

7777 W. BLUEMOUND RD. P.O. BOX 13819 MILWAUKEE, WI 53213

Prices, contents, and availability subject to change without notice.
Disney characters and artwork © Disney Enterprises, Inc.

0616